FROM THE CREATOR OF
H★MILTON
AND THE DIRECTOR OF
CRAZY·RICH·ASIANS

MUSIC FROM THE ORIGINAL MOTION PICTURE

In The Heights

Piraguas

MUSIC AND LYRICS BY
LIN-MANUEL MIRANDA

Alfred

alfred.com

Printed in USA.

ISBN-10: 1-4706-4814-8   ISBN-13: 978-1-4706-4814-5

THE TIME
HAS COME

In The
Heights

In The Heights

CONTENTS

IN THE HEIGHTS 6

BREATHE 31

¡NO ME DIGA! 45

IT WON'T BE LONG NOW 55

96,000 68

PIRAGUA 91

WHEN YOU'RE HOME 97

BLACKOUT 114

¡PACIENCIA Y FE! 130

ALABANZA 146

WHEN THE SUN GOES DOWN 153

CHAMPAGNE 159

HOME ALL SUMMER 169

IN THE HEIGHTS

Music and Lyrics by LIN-MANUEL MIRANDA
Arranged by ALEX LACAMOIRE
and BILL SHERMAN

USNAVI:

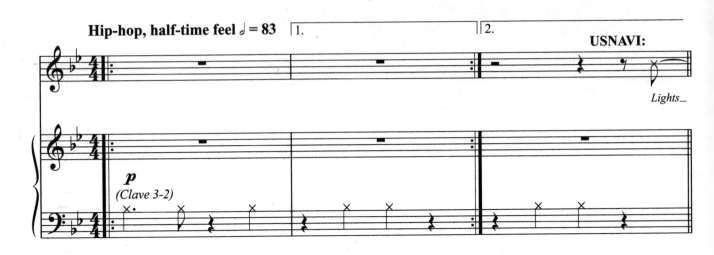

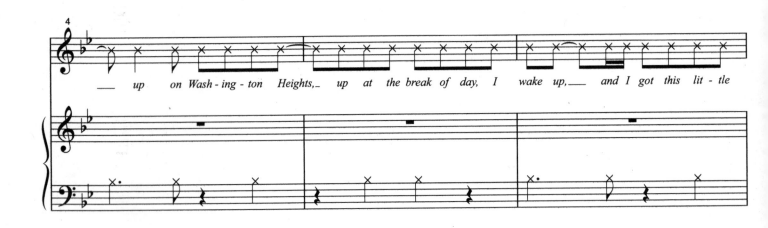

up on Wash-ing-ton Heights,_ up at the break of day, I wake up,_ and I got this lit - tle

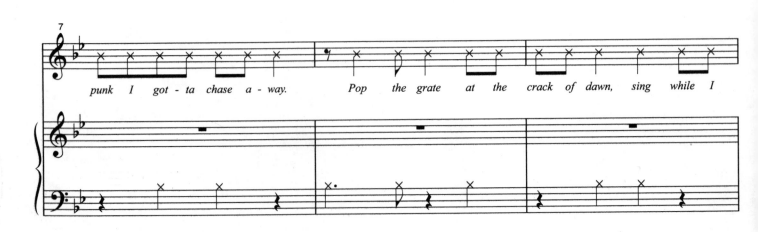

punk I got - ta chase a - way. Pop the grate at the crack of dawn, sing while I

PIRAGUA GUY: *"Ice cold piragua! Parcha. China.*
Cherry. Strawberry. And just for today, I got mamey!"
USNAVI: *"Oye, Piragü, ¿Cómo estás?"*
3x **PIRAGUA GUY:** *"Como siempre, Señor Usnavi."*

D
F♯7
Bm
F/G
C
134
USNAVI: "Sonny, you're late!"
SONNY: "Chillax, you know you love me."
sub. p
mf
f
E7
Am
F
F/G
138
USNAVI:
Me and my cous - in run - nin' just an - oth - er dime - a - doz - en Mom - and - Pop Stop - and - Shop. And, oh my God, it's got - ten
mf
C
E7
Am
F
F/G
142
too darn hot, like my man Cole Por - ter said. Peo - ple come through for a few cold wa - ters and a
sub. f
mf
C
E7
Am
F
F/G
146
lot - ter - y tick - et, just a part of the rou - tine. Ev - 'ry - bod - y's got a job, ev - 'ry - bod - y's got a dream. They

22

Pon de replay dance beat (swing 8ths continue)

Esus
E
Am/E
308
(with COMMUNITY:)
the late nights! You'll taste beans and rice! The syr - up and shaved ice! I ain't
Heights! In the Heights!
fp
cresc. poco a poco
E
F/E
311
gon - na say it twice. Turn up the street lights, we're tak - in' a flight to a cou - ple of
In the Heights! Ah, ah, ah,
mf
E7sus
N.C.
Am
314
days in the life of what it's like. En Wash - ing - ton Heights!
ah! En Wash - ing - ton Heights!
f
ff
sffz

BREATHE

Music and Lyrics by LIN-MANUEL MIRANDA
*Arranged by ALEX LACAMOIRE
and BILL SHERMAN*

PIRAGUA GUY:

Si - gue_an - dan - do_el ca - mi - no por to - da su vi - da._____ Res - pi - ra..._____

¡NO ME DIGA!

Music and Lyrics by LIN-MANUEL MIRANDA
Arranged by ALEX LACAMOIRE
and BILL SHERMAN

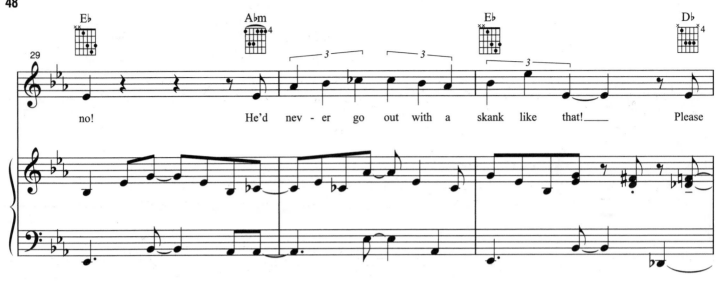

no! He'd nev - er go out with a skank like that!____ Please

DANIELA:

tell me you're jok - ing! O - kay! Just want - ed to see____ what you'd

LADIES:

say! Tell me some - thing I____ don't know!_

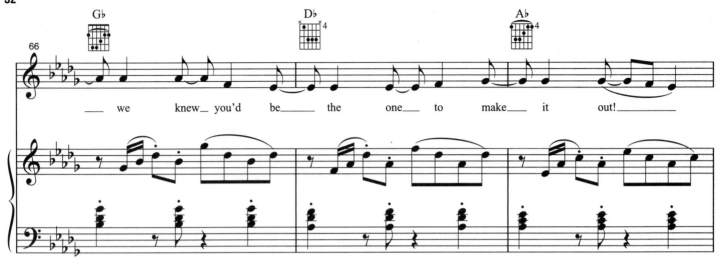

we knew__ you'd be__ the one__ to make__ it out!_____

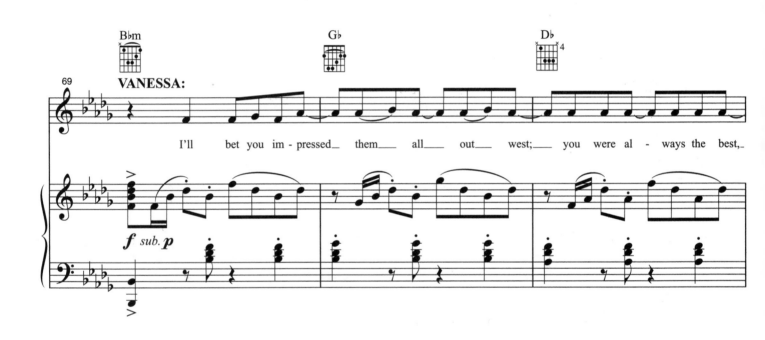

VANESSA:

I'll bet you im - pressed__ them__ all__ out__ west;__ you were al - ways the best,__

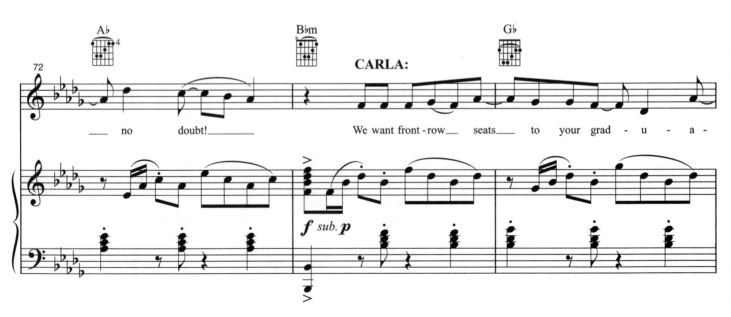

CARLA:

__ no doubt!_____ We want front - row__ seats__ to your grad - u - a -

DANIELA:

I don't know!

CARLA/VANESSA/CUCA:

Tell me

some - thing I don't know!____ ¿Qué sé yo? ¿Qué sé yo?

IT WON'T BE LONG NOW

Music and Lyrics by LIN-MANUEL MIRANDA
Arranged by ALEX LACAMOIRE
and BILL SHERMAN

It Won't Be Long Now - 13 - 1

VANESSA:

I'm run-ning to make it home,__ and home's__ what Va-nes-sa's run-ning a-way from. The

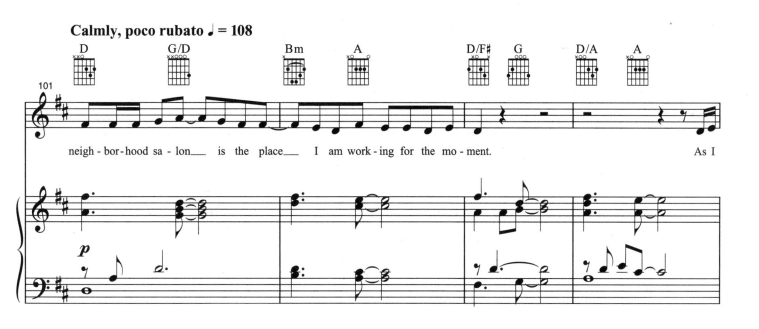

Calmly, poco rubato ♩ = 108

neigh-bor-hood sa-lon__ is the place__ I am work-ing for the mo-ment. As I

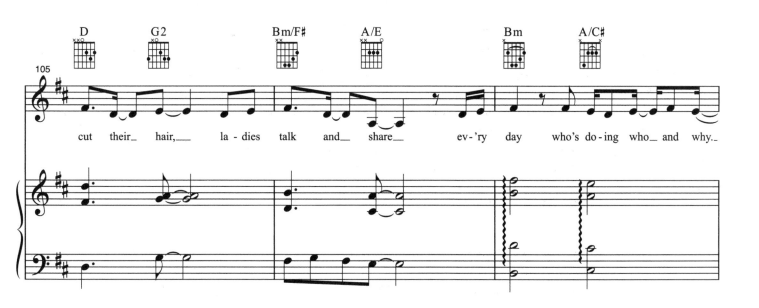

cut their__ hair,__ la-dies talk and__ share__ ev-'ry day who's do-ing who__ and why.__

96,000

Music and Lyrics by LIN-MANUEL MIRANDA
Arranged by ALEX LACAMOIRE
and BILL SHERMAN

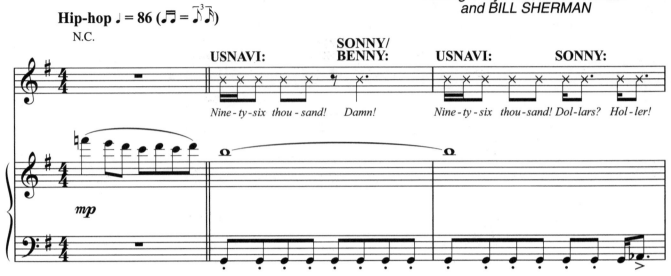

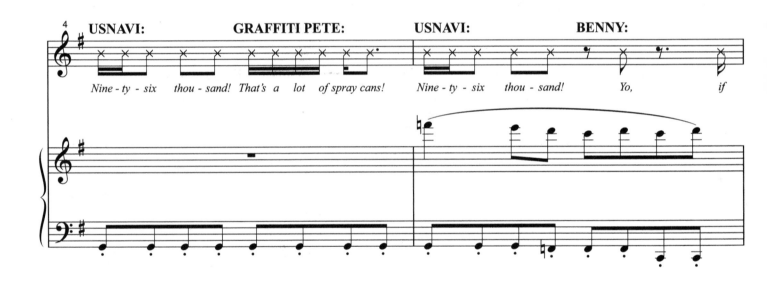

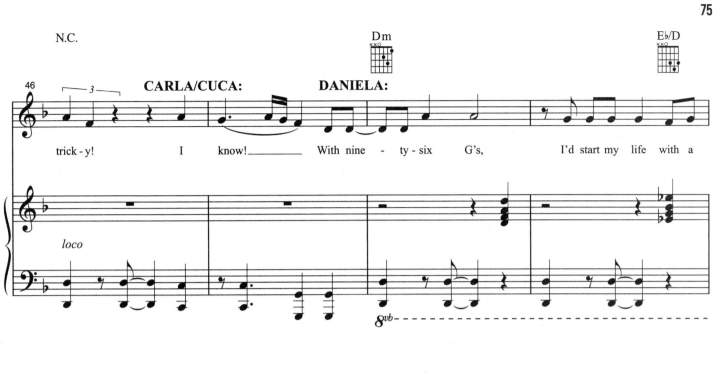

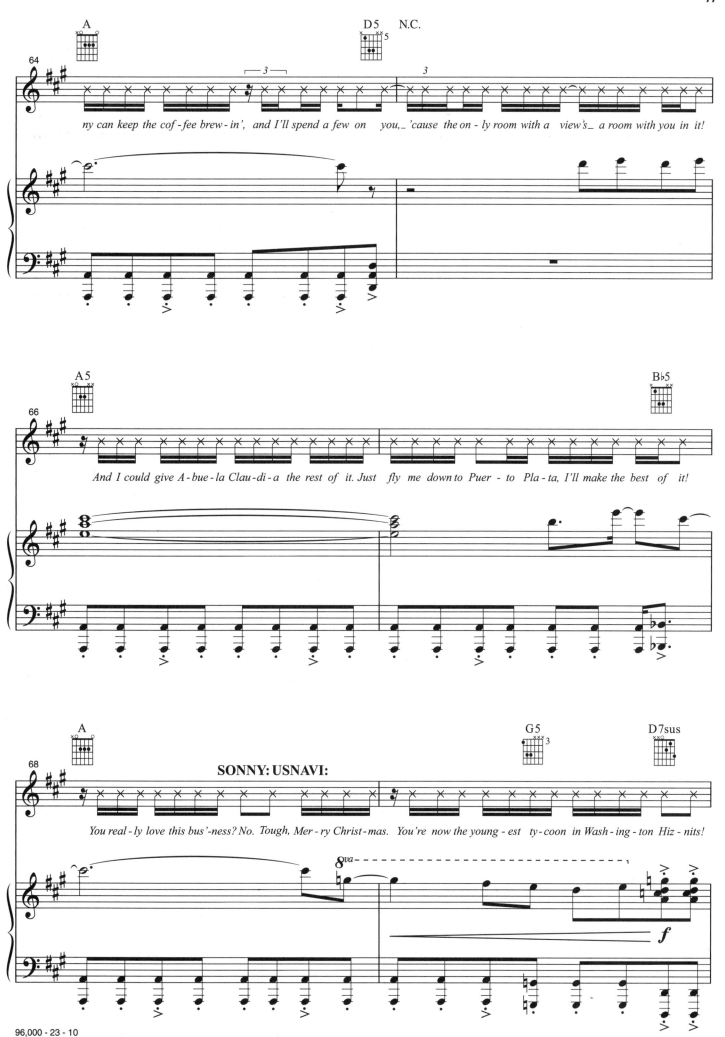

PIRAGUA

Music and Lyrics by LIN-MANUEL MIRANDA
*Arranged by ALEX LACAMOIRE
and BILL SHERMAN*

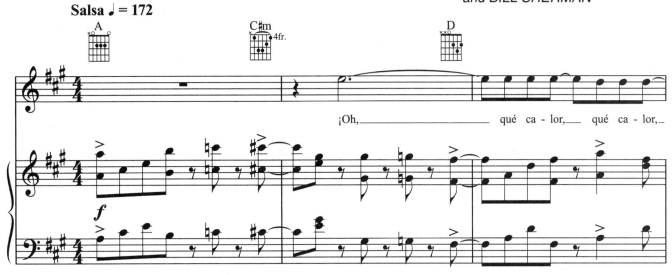

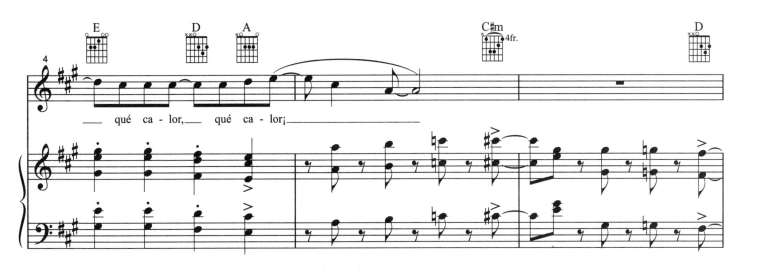

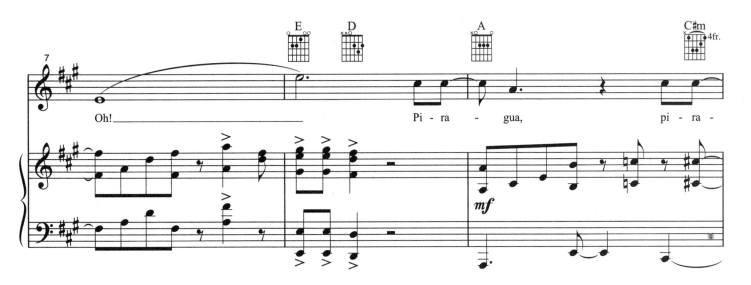

Piragua - 6 - 1

WHEN YOU'RE HOME

Music and Lyrics by LIN-MANUEL MIRANDA
*Arranged by ALEX LACAMOIRE
and BILL SHERMAN*

NINA:
I used to think we lived at the top of the world, when the world was just a sub-way map. And the One-slash-Nine climbed a dot-ted line to my place.

BENNY:
There's no Nine train now.

NINA:
Right.

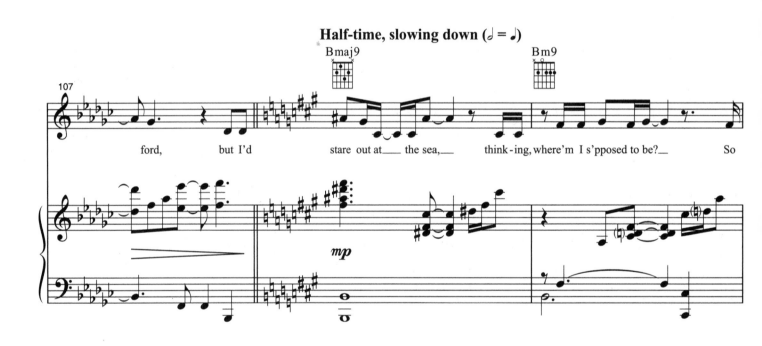

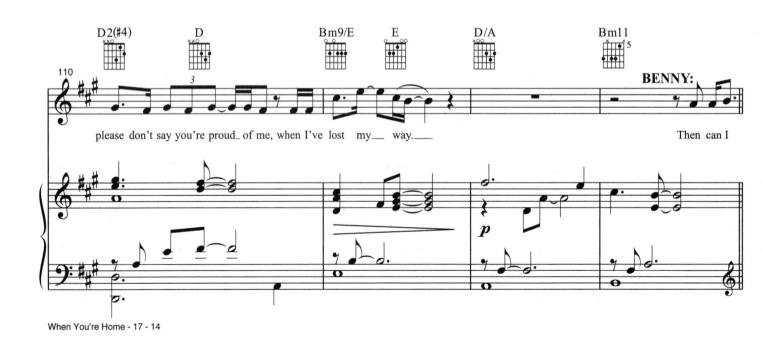

BLACKOUT

Music and Lyrics by LIN-MANUEL MIRANDA
*Arranged by ALEX LACAMOIRE
and BILL SHERMAN*

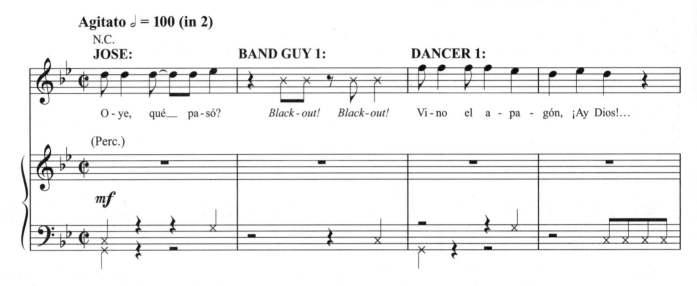

SONNY/CLUBGOERS:

Gm
E♭
Dm
F
Fsus
F
53
ENSEMBLE:
Look at the fi - re-works... Look at the fi - re-works fly!
Look at the fi - re-works...
mf
Gm
E♭2
B♭
F
57
Light up the night sky!
Light up the night sky!
Gm
E♭
Dm
F
Fsus
F
61
Look at the fi - re-works fly!
Look at the fi - re-works...
f

Look at the fi - re - works...

Look at the fi - re - works... Look at the fi - re - works...

Look at the fi - re - works...

¡PACIENCIA Y FE!

Music and Lyrics by LIN-MANUEL MIRANDA
*Arranged by ALEX LACAMOIRE
and BILL SHERMAN*

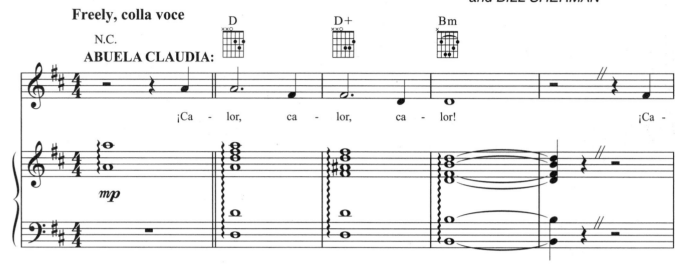

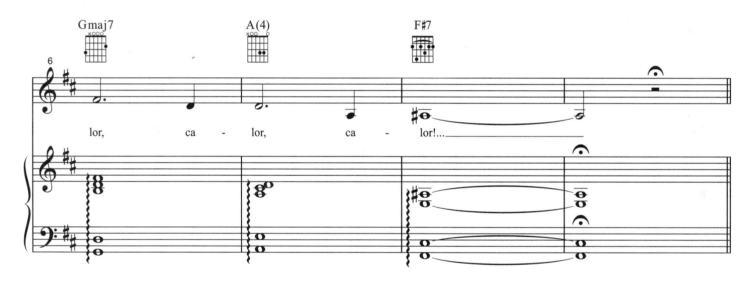

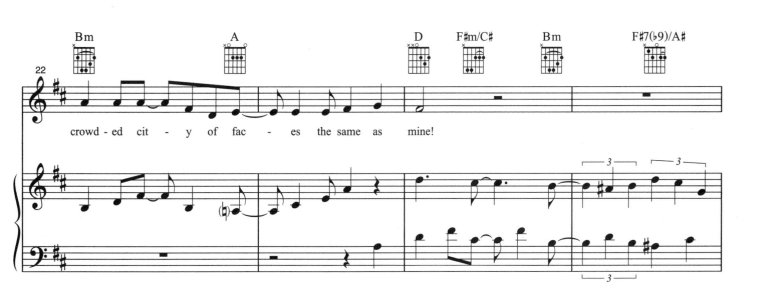

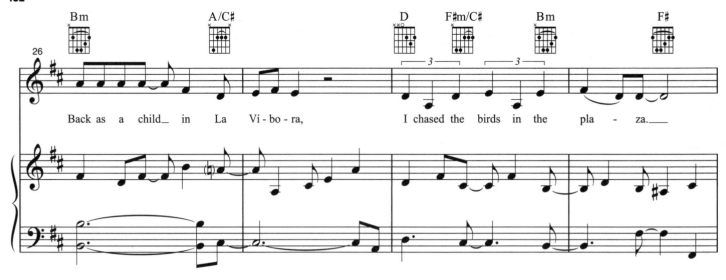

Back as a child__ in La Ví - bo - ra, I chased the birds in the pla - za.__

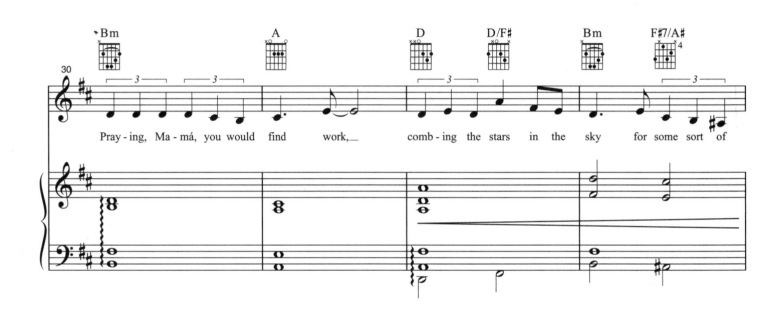

Pray - ing, Ma - má, you would find work,__ comb - ing the stars in the sky for some sort of

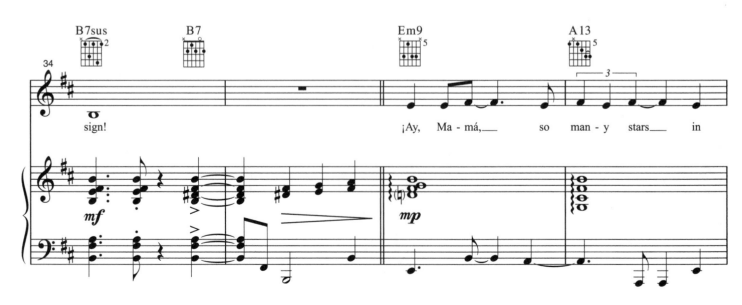

sign! ¡Ay, Ma - má,__ so man - y stars__ in

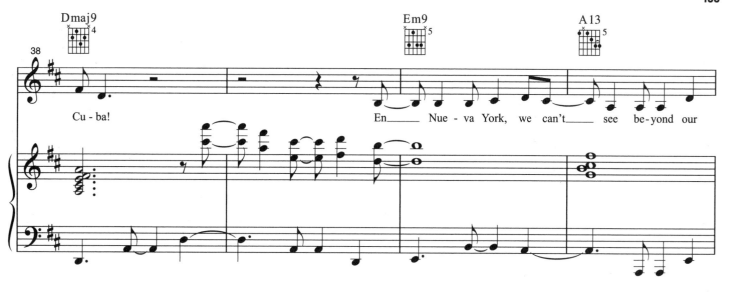

Cu - ba! En___ Nue - va York, we can't___ see be - yond our

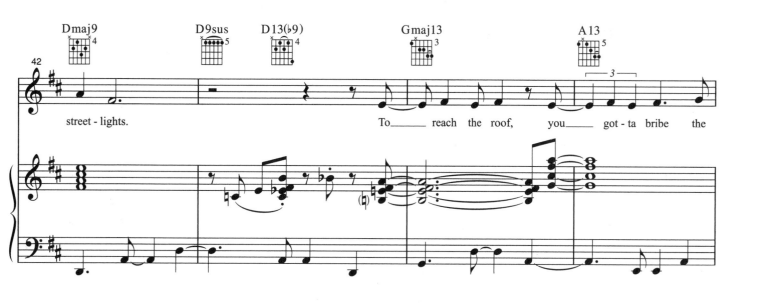

street - lights. To___ reach the roof, you___ got - ta bribe the

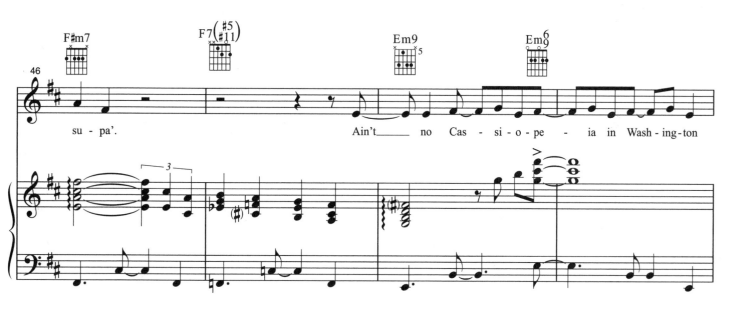

su - pa'. Ain't___ no Cas - si - o - pe - ia in Wash - ing - ton

¡Paciencia y Fe! - 16 - 4

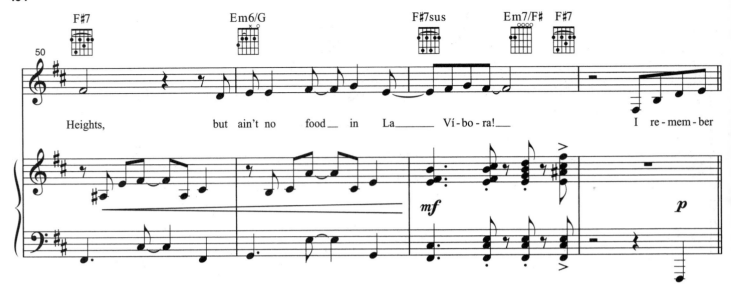

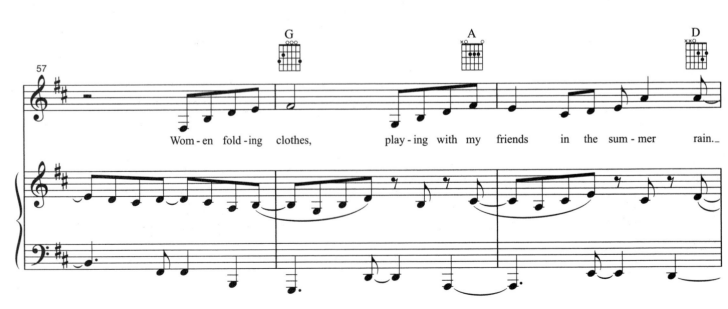

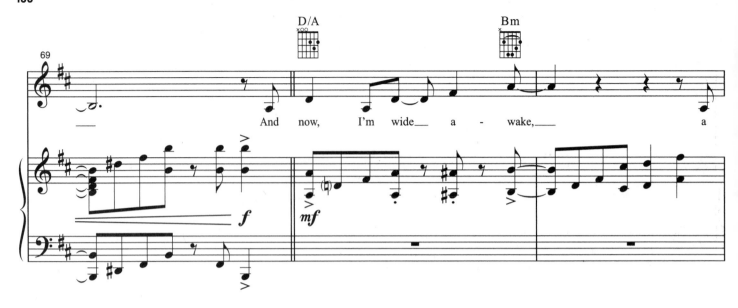

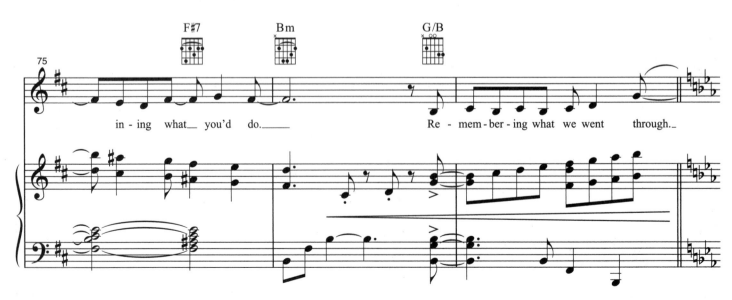

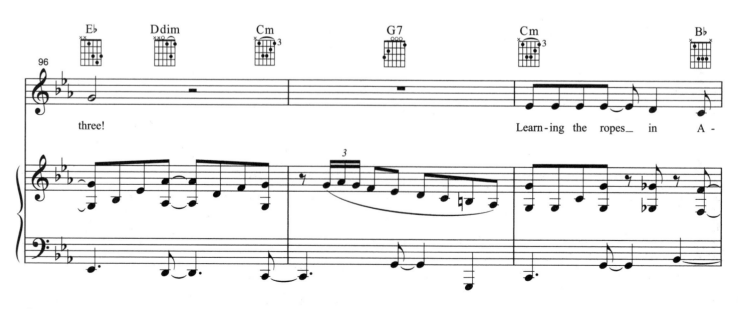

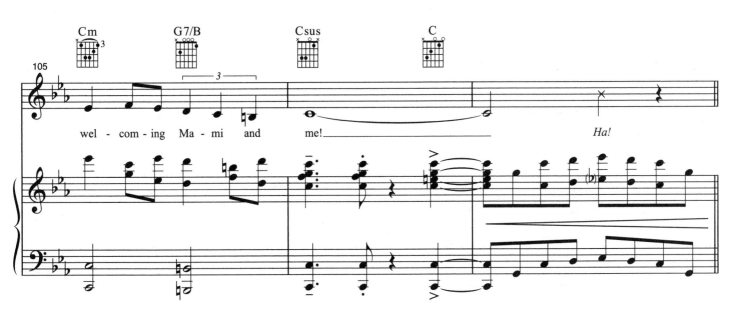

ALABANZA

Music and Lyrics by LIN-MANUEL MIRANDA
*Arranged by ALEX LACAMOIRE
and BILL SHERMAN*

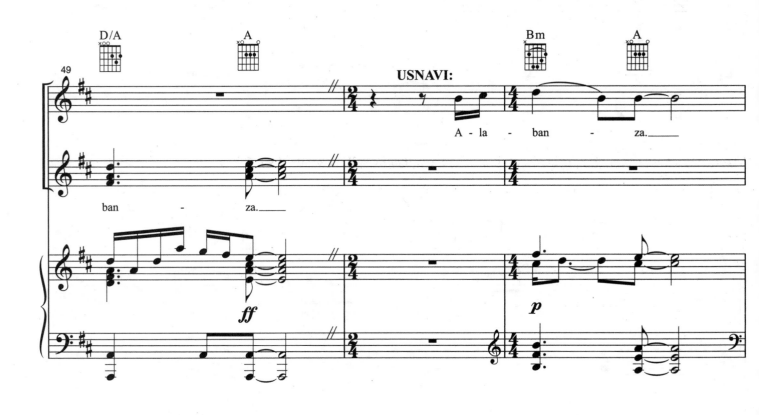

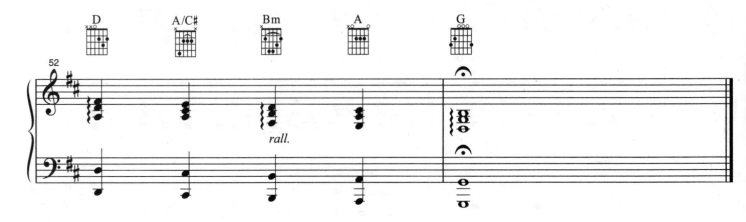

WHEN THE SUN GOES DOWN

Music and Lyrics by LIN-MANUEL MIRANDA
Arranged by ALEX LACAMOIRE
and BILL SHERMAN

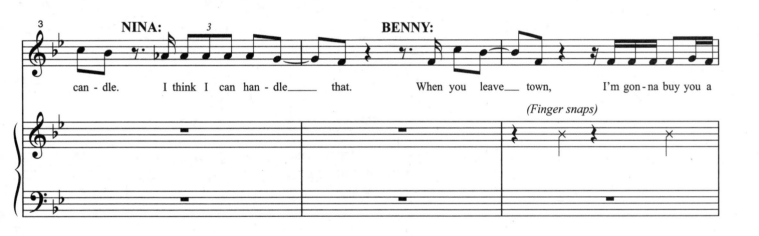

When the Sun Goes Down - 6 - 1

CHAMPAGNE

Music and Lyrics by LIN-MANUEL MIRANDA
Arranged by ALEX LACAMOIRE
and BILL SHERMAN

Moderately ♩ = 92

VANESSA: So I got you a pres-ent... I went next door to get it...

Do-ing an-y-thing to-night? You're done for the

USNAVI: Clean-ing.

day. 'Cuz we got a date. Be-fore you

No way. O-kay.

HOME ALL SUMMER

Music and Lyrics by
LIN-MANUEL MIRANDA
Arranged by
LIN-MANUEL MIRANDA and TROOKO

170

Home All Summer - 12 - 2

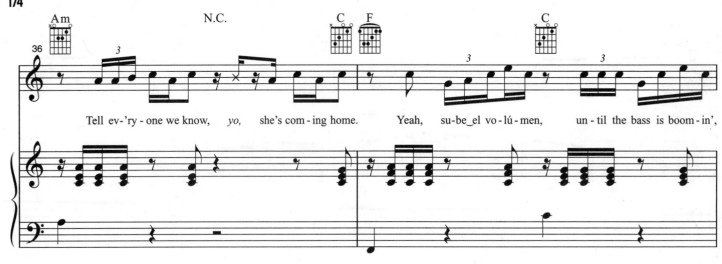

Tell ev-'ry-one we know, yo, she's com-ing home. Yeah, su-be el vo-lú-men, un-til the bass is boom-in',

USNAVI/NINA:

un-till the place is mov-in', un-til the fac-es in the room are me and you, what it do. I'll be here all

Chorus:

sum-mer. I'll be here all sum-mer. If you're gon-na be a-

COMPANY:

Yeah,__ yeah,__ yeah, yeah.__ Yeah,__ yeah,__ yeah, yeah.__